Connor,

Become what you are,

Alex 2022

COACHED
BY
JOAN OF ARC

COACHED BY JOAN OF ARC

Lessons in Virtuous Leadership

ALEXANDRE HAVARD

Scepter

Translation from French by Anthony Salvia

Alexandre Havard created the Virtuous Leadership system, which is now taught in countries the world over. His books *Virtuous Leadership* (2007), *Created for Greatness* (2011), *From Temperament to Character* (2018), and *Free Hearts* (2019) have been translated into some twenty languages. After graduating from Paris Descartes University with a degree in law, he served as a barrister in Strasbourg and Helsinki. He is the founder of the Virtuous Leadership Institute, which has affiliates in numerous countries on five continents.

There are many Christians who are persuaded that the Redemption will be completed in all environments of the world, and that there have to be some souls—they do not know which ones—who will contribute to carrying it out with Christ. But they think it will take centuries, many centuries. It would be an eternity, if it were to take place at the rate of their self-giving. That was the way you yourself thought, until someone came to "wake you up."

–St. Josemaría Escrivá, *Furrow*

An Encounter

An insipid-looking girl mounted on a muscular war horse, nearly asphyxiated and crushed by her armor—that was the way I imagined Joan of Arc during my years at school and in college. Joan of Arc did not move me at all. After all, it was no longer the patriotic time of 1914. Rather, it was "The Deserter," written by the eccentric Boris Vian and sung by the very melancholic Serge Reggiani, which I retain in my memory from that time. His magnificent despair grabbed me in the gut.

Joan of Arc entered into my life at the turn of the millennium. I was approaching my forties. I had been living in Finland for more than ten years. France was far away. And suddenly, in the icy darkness of a winter's night very much like so many others, I perceived a face radiating light and purity!

The face of Joan. A smiling, rather mischievous face said to me, "Let's go." She said it in English. These words resonated in the deepest, most intimate part of my soul with a power preventing me from doubting for a single instant.

A grace of God—I have never had the slightest doubt, so much had her presence filled me with joy and peace. This grace led me to give up the practice of law and devote myself to the teaching of virtuous leadership all over the world.

Contents

Preface

In October 2017, at the end of a conference on virtuous leadership I was giving in Ottawa, a young Canadian came up to me and asked, "How do you become Joan of Arc?"

He clearly meant it as a serious question. I sensed in him a deep anxiety, a sincere emotion. He was a big, burly guy with a thick red beard. A lumberjack, perhaps. . . .

I did not have time to answer his question. I could see that a long queue of people wanting me to sign copies of my book had formed behind him. We would have had to sit down in a quiet corner with several bottles of vodka and cartons of raw herring before discussing this exceptional figure of French history, who, according to Mark Twain, "is easily and by far the most extraordinary person the human race has ever produced."[1]

The next day I returned to Europe and thought that one day I would have to write not a biography of Joan—there are already hundreds of very interesting and well-docu-

---

1 Mark Twain, *Personal Recollections of Joan of Arc* (1896; repr., Mineola, N.Y.: Dover, 2002), p. 329.

mented books about the heroine of Orléans—but a work responding to the eminently practical question posed by my Canadian: "How do you become Joan of Arc?"

Later, I understood that the best way to do this would be to let Joan coach us, take us by the hand and whisper some wise counsel in our ear—counsel that would be relevant for both young people and adults, counsel stemming from her life, which was no less heroic than her death.

It is not a question of actually becoming Joan of Arc. Joan was a unique and inimitable personage. To try to reproduce her in our life would be a big mistake. This would be limiting God in his capacity to innovate and erecting obstacles to his creativity and imagination. Rather, it is a question of profiting from Joan's wisdom, which even today captivates men and women of goodwill and envelops her in mystery.

Washington, De Gaulle, Churchill . . . , these illustrious war leaders also have something to say to us, but it is hard to imagine engaging in an intimate dialogue with them. This is not because these great men were mediocrities compared to Joan. No, it is just that their hearts, no matter their personal nobility, were not of the same substance.

Joan is a masterpiece, whose beauty provokes in us sublime emotions bursting the boundaries of our being and propelling us to unexpected heights. In contemplating Joan—her personality, her deeds, and her words—the straitjacket of our quietude and mediocrity falls away in euphoric wonder. Joan conveys to us the beauty and the greatness of the human being and arouses in us a thirst for life, for engagement, and for sacrifice.

In a world dominated by the religion of the belly, Joan is a beacon in the night.

Author's Note

Those having only a superficial knowledge of Joan's life may wish to begin by consulting the chronology at the end of the book. Doing so will help in understanding the events to which Joan is referring as she advises us.

Ingres, Jean Auguste Dominique, *Joan of Arc
at the Coronation of Charles VII in Reims* (detail),
oil on canvas, 1854, Louvre, Paris, France.

One

Finding Victory in Defeat

You have just suffered a defeat and are unhappy.
You do not understand.
This setback did not figure in your plans.

No one likes what the world calls "defeat."

I also did not appreciate being held prisoner in Compiègne and being reduced to ashes in Rouen before my mission had been completed. The English were still in France and the king had yet not entered Paris when I died at the stake.

Nevertheless, thanks to my martyrdom, I achieved my mission. As my ordeal was unfolding, the English began to doubt they would prevail. "We are all lost. We have burned a saint!" These horrified proclamations were exclaimed by the most clairvoyant in the entourage of the

King of England. The morale of the enemy was shaken. But above all—and this is the important thing—through my ordeal I won the hearts of thousands of men and women; I acquired a strength both spiritual and material, which could not be stopped. My soldiers, from that day on, began to fight not "with me," as previously, but "for me." My men will achieve my mission.

"My men will achieve it!" If you only knew the joy with which I utter these words. I loved people more than things, more than strategies, and more than "sacred" goals. My mission became *their* mission. My strength became *their* strength.

Through my martyrdom, I achieved my mission. Who could have foreseen it? Everyone thought it was the end of a beautiful adventure, whereas it was just the beginning. Five years later, the English lost Paris, and soon thereafter, the rest of the kingdom.

The English wanted to do more than take my life; by having me condemned as a heretic, they wanted to tarnish my memory, to discredit my cause and thereby the King of France, who owed his crown to me. But without realizing it, they erected a monument—the record of my trial—which no one could challenge because it was their handiwork. Without this monument, I would be more a legend than a reality. No one would have given glory to God for the marvels he did in me, and no one would have learned of my virtues. It is thanks to my trial, and this testimony—the like of which history had never seen—that today I continue to work in the hearts of men. It is thanks to my judges, to the often absurd and humiliating questions they posed, that the whole world knows of my life and spirit. Bishop Pierre Cauchon, the head of the tribunal and the main negotiator of the Treaty of Troyes, which gave France to the English, wanted to preside over a "beautiful trial," as he said. And it is because he wanted the trial to be "beautiful" that my words were recorded, timed, and sealed. He wanted to tarnish my memory forever, but the more he tarnished it, the more it served the plans of God. Unknowingly, he was building a monument to my glory.

During the trial, the moment came when, exhausted, I did not want to answer any more questions. I was not aware that my answers were my triumph. But God knew it, which is why he ordered me to *boldly* and tirelessly answer all of the questions of the judges. That is what I did.

Put your trust in God, as I trusted in him. Where you see defeat, God sees victory. You cannot always discern the profound meaning of events. Subordinate your intelligence to his providence.

I know subordinating our intelligence is a hard thing for adults to do. You have to have humility and make yourself small in order to become a child. I was always a child before God, even when I was leading armies and mixing with the great ones of this world. I never thought like an adult. That is why adults liked to see me and listened to me. They saw in me an invincible strength, which is nothing other than the trust of a child in his father. They did not understand this trust—they were too old for that—but it had the power to bring them to their knees and often made them cry.

So do not fear defeat. If your motives are pure, if your means are just, if you put yourself into what you are doing, and if you persevere, then leave the outcome in the hands of God. Do not let anxiety devastate your spirit.

Some practical advice:
Identify three major defeats in your life and discover in them all of the victories you derived or could have derived from them: 1) for your personal growth; 2) for the benefit of others; 3) for the quality of your professional, familial, and social life.

Mote, W.H., *Joan of Arc* (detail),
Engraving, 1858,
published in "World Noted Women," USA.

Two

Be Aware of Your Strength

You trust in God.
But you have insufficient trust in yourself.

Since early childhood, you were told that we should trust in God, not in ourselves. But if God trusts you, is it right that you do not trust yourself? If God rejoices in the talents he gave you, should you not do the same?

In trusting your talents, you are trusting God, who gave them to you.

I was confident in my talents. Everyone who knew me agreed that I was tall and beautiful, strong and at the same time profoundly feminine. I had a soft voice and spoke in a way admired by others. I was sensitive and did not hide my tears. I liked to laugh and make others laugh. I had a proud look and a joyous face. I took care over my appearance when necessary. I had a religious soul in a robust, magnificent, and healthy body. I was conscious of all of these gifts, of all of these qualities of body and spirit.

I wanted to live life to the fullest. I wanted to scale the heights of my humanity and realize my greatest potential. Listen to what Sir Winston Churchill said about me, "Joan was a being so uplifted from the ordinary run of mankind that she finds no equal in a thousand years."[2]

In recognizing our talents, we give thanks to God, who created us. Refusing to recognize our talents is not humility but ingratitude. Recognizing our talents, increasing them, and using them well is the virtue of magnanimity, the virtue of the great.

And I, who was a child before God, never ceased multiplying the gifts I had received. I was great, tremendous, and magnanimous. This magnanimity stimulated hope in me, rendering it engaging, exalting, and intoxicating. It impelled me to action. Before the task at hand, my heart swelled, my soul found its impetus, and my body rose above all difficulties.

I trusted in God, but I also trusted in myself. My human hope was commensurate with the superhuman, supernatural hope, which God placed in my soul the day I was baptized.

---

2   Winston Churchill, *The Birth of Britain*, vol. 1 of *A History of the English Speaking Peoples* (New York: Dodd, Mead & Co., 1956), p. 422.

I expected everything of God as if I could do nothing myself, and I expected everything of myself as if God did not exist. I was a child before God, but a giant before men.

With me, the immensity of the human was not swallowed up by the immensity of grace.

Recall what G. K. Chesterton wrote about me:

> Joan of Arc was not stuck at the cross-roads, either by rejecting all the paths like Tolstoy, or by accepting them all like Nietzsche. She chose a path and went down it like a thunderbolt . . . . Tolstoy only *praised* the peasant; she *was* the peasant. Nietzsche only *praised* the warrior; she *was* the warrior. She beat them both at their own antagonistic ideals; she was more gentle than the one, more violent than the other.[3]

I was violent like a thunderbolt.

Mounting a horse and leading armies did not make me a "superwoman." I was not a Hollywood creation. In battle, I never killed anyone; I used only my standard. I was not a would-be man. What *did* make me a "superwoman" was that I developed my feminine nature to the fullest.

I was so much a woman that Voltaire, vexed, was moved to tears of hatred. This horrid man saw me as the incarnation of Christian humanism, the one which

3   G. K. Chesterton, *Orthodoxy* (New York: John Lane, 1908), p. 79.

exposed the inconsistency of all his theories. Daughters of men, who are also daughters of God, horrify the enemies of Jesus Christ. They are too beautiful to pass unnoticed. I was truly beautiful. In my beauty, Voltaire became aware of his ugliness and he wrote a pamphlet—*The Maid of Orleans*—in which he devoted eight thousand verses to attacking my honor.

Schiller came to my defense. "O Virgin, mockery has dragged you through the muck . . . . But have no fear, there still exist beautiful souls enflamed by greatness."[4] But it was above all the poet Aleksandr Pushkin, who came to my aid and restored my honor. Several hours before his death in Saint Petersburg in 1837, he wrote these words in what turned out to be his final work:

> There is no subject in modern history more moving and more poetic than the life and death of the heroine of Orléans. What did Voltaire, this worthy representative of the French people, do with it? Just once in his life it was given to him to be a poet and this is how he used his inspiration! With his satanic breath he fans the dying flames amidst the ashes of the stake, and like a drunken savage he dances around his miserable bonfire. Like the Roman executioners of long ago, he adds insults to the mortal suffering of the Virgin . . . .

4   Friedrich von Schiller, *Die Jungfrau von Orleans* (1801).

Everyone in France enthusiastically received this book in which contempt for everything held sacred by man and the citizen reaches the heights of cynicism. What a sad century! What a sad people.[5]

What a gentleman, this Russian! At the moment of his death—he died in a duel—I asked God to grant him the grace of repentance, and he did. I owed him that.

This is what I wanted to tell you today. Be aware of your talents. Multiply them. Live at full tilt. May your humility not be pusillanimity! May your humility never deviate from your magnanimity! Develop your human potential to the point of exhaustion, and do not be afraid of humanists spewing hatred.

Some practical advice:

Make a list of talents—physical, spiritual, cultural—which you have received from God, from your parents, grandparents, brothers, sisters, and friends. Consider the talents that stem from your physiological temperament: for the choleric, action; for the melancholic, creativity; for the sanguine, communication; for the phlegmatic, rational thinking. "What am I strong in?" Ask your parents, friends, and professors. Try to multiply these talents at work, in the family, and in social life.

---

5   A. Pushkin, *Posledniy iz svojstvennikov Ioanny d'Ark* (1837).

Bénouville, Léon-François, *Joan of Arc Listening to Her Voices* (detail), oil on canvas, c.1859, Musée des Beaux-arts de Rouen, Rouen, France.

Three

Magnanimity Trumps Self-Esteem

*You are aware of your talents
and are doing everything to grow them.
But you are having doubts;
wagging tongues are saying you lack humility.*

Do not worry. Many have a false understanding of humility. Humility is the virtue of those who live in the truth of who they are. And the truth is that you have received talents, which must bear fruit. Thus, humility goes hand in hand with magnanimity.

Magnanimity is a concept coming from the Greeks, which the Roman humanist Cicero forged for the West several decades before the birth of Christ. Magnanimity is the virtue of those who consider themselves capable of great things and who affirm their dignity and greatness through their words and deeds.

Much has been said about humility in order to emphasize this great truth: God is the *source* of all good. But less has been said about magnanimity and the *greatness* of the good we have been given. The source of this good is of interest to many, but the good itself gets overlooked. It is believed that magnanimity overshadows humility. This is a grave theoretical mistake; if humility is the virtue of those living in the truth about themselves, magnanimity—the virtue of those who are aware of their dignity and greatness—is an integral part of this humility, of this truth. The truth about the source of greatness must not hide the truth about greatness as such.

Acknowledging your dignity and greatness is an act of humility because it leads you to the truth about yourself.

You will say to me, "What about modesty?" Modesty should not be an obstacle to humility. Humility is more important than modesty. Recall the words of C. S. Lewis, "Perfect humility dispenses with modesty; if God is satisfied with the work, the work may be satisfied with itself."[6]

Did you know that my voices called me, "Daughter

---

6   C. S. Lewis, *The Weight of Glory and Other Addresses* (1941, repr. New York: HarperOne, 2001), p. 38.

of God"? They said, "Go, Daughter of God." I trembled when I heard these words. Trembled with joy. I collapsed in ecstasy every time I heard them. Because I am a daughter of God, I embarked on this adventure. It was a sense of my personal dignity, which pushed me to act. "I am a daughter of God and I will kick the English out of France. This is what I was born for." These are the words I liked to repeat and with which I affirmed my dignity. Some thought this was pride. They were wrong, because it was true. Others said it showed a lack of modesty. They were right; I was too humble to have any interest in mere modesty.

To think that magnanimity puts humility in the shade is a grave theoretical error. But the practical consequences of this error are even graver: to cede the terrain of greatness to unbelievers, agnostics, and atheists is to leave in their hands this world ransomed by Christ for the sons and daughters of God. How wretched and what a travesty of justice!

We have been talking about humility in the wrong way. It is true that man by himself is absolute nothingness, a non-being, but the man who was created in the image of God, ransomed by the Son and divinized by the Holy Spirit, is a true wonder. Man was constituted as a son of God. This intimate truth, this sublime reality, should impel you to accomplish great things. You are a son of

God—there is no greater dignity than that. This dignity should encourage you to dream and convert your dream into a mission.

There is a lot of talk these days of "self-esteem." But you no more need self-esteem than you need modesty. Magnanimity and self-esteem are two very different things. Magnanimity is a virtue, a spiritual habit; self-esteem is a feeling of a psychological kind. A virtue is something stable and objective; a feeling can be very unstable and is always subjective. You can get up in the morning feeling a powerful sense of self-esteem and go to bed at night feeling like a total failure. A pusillanimous person can have an overflowing self-esteem; a magnanimous person can have very limited self-esteem. *Feeling* our greatness (self-esteem) is not the same thing as *being aware* of our greatness (magnanimity). You do not need to know yourself in order to feel yourself great—flattery can suffice to do that for you. Magnanimity is the result of knowing oneself, whereas self-esteem depends mainly on how others perceive us.

Remember: you need humility more than modesty and magnanimity more than self-esteem.

Some practical advice:
Identify the moments in your life when you were paralyzed by modesty. "Who am I to want to save the world . . . others are more capable than I am . . . I'm no genius, I

didn't study at Harvard or Stanford . . . I am not a super-man; I am not a star . . . I am a good boy or a nice girl, but nothing more." Get a grip on yourself. Contemplate your moments of pusillanimity or mendacity, when you lost sight of your dignity and your talents. Correct those things, if you still can. Above all, impress upon yourself this conviction: despair is worse than presumption, believing yourself capable of certain things when you are not, because it condemns you to mediocrity and degradation. If by temperament you are phlegmatic, this piece of advice will be harder to act on than for others, because you tend to underestimate your talents, to settle into a routine, to easily accept the *status quo*. Do not be discouraged. Learn to dream. Many phlegmatic persons have had remarkable success in practicing magnanimity.

Unknown artist, Joan of Arc (detail), 1800s, bronze, Nanterre, France.

Four

Create a Plan for Personal Growth

You ask me what to do to become great.

I tell you:

Identify in the course of this year several magnanimous people you would like to meet. Seek out their company. Contemplate them. Learn from them to dream, decide, and act. Study the lives of history's noblest personalities.

Study me.

Create a magnanimous environment around you. Your environment is the books you read, the movies you watch, the images you contemplate, and the music you listen to. It is the internet with all its greatness and vileness. Be selective: reject what is morally dubious and fill your heart and mind with noble and beautiful things.

I lived in a world very different from yours. We had fewer temptations. Your temptations are artificial. They are generated by ideology and commerce. They manipulate you, morning, noon, and night. Do not let yourself be manipulated. It is true that man is a social being, who cannot and should not escape influences. Choose what influences you want for yourself—the positive ones you need. Make plans for yourself and your family and follow them.

I grew up in a supportive atmosphere, which my parents created for me and that I freely accepted as an adult. In this atmosphere, I made great strides without knowing it. I was lucky, of course, to have virtuous parents. During adolescence, I could have thrown everything I had received out the window but did not. I kept it all.

So, remember these words: magnanimous environment, positive influences, and supportive atmosphere. Be intelligent enough to create such an environment and strong enough not to abandon it.

Learn to experience the greatness of ordinary life. Contemplate everything noble within it.

Growing up, I sensed the greatness in the little things of daily life. I did not go to school but helped my mother sew, do the laundry, and cook. Sometimes I worked in the stable or in the fields, using, according to my father's wish, either the harrow or the plow, or looked after the flock in the communal meadow. I saw how my mother prepared meals. Through her cooking, she elevated us not just physically but spiritually. Through her talent, which was a manifestation of greatness, she gave us all a sense of our own dignity and encouraged us always to give the best of ourselves.

Be astonished by things greater than yourself.

Many things delighted me: nature, plants, animals, and the hard work of the men and women of Domrémy. I was easily moved by beauty, goodness, and virtue, without trying to reduce realities to my poor ability to understand. I did not try to "comprehend," to contain, or to possess. Instead, I let myself be astonished, seized, and embraced by what was greater than me. I learned to contemplate beauty, to marvel at it, and respond to it in the right way. My free heart became accustomed to saying *yes* to the divine impulses and inspirations manifesting themselves in the depths of my being. I opened my heart to transcendence. I learned to let myself be loved before I learned to love. I learned to contemplate before learning to act.

Make a daily plan for spiritual and cultural growth, setting precise times for meditation, reading, and sports.

I went to church every day to attend the Holy Sacrifice. I prostrated myself before the cross. I spoke to Jesus and Mary. In the evening, when the bell chiming compline surprised me in the field, I genuflected, and raised my soul to God. I did these things not from time to time but every day. It is the regular rhythm of life, not the fleeting moment of emotions, which forges character and educates the heart.

Do not compare yourself to anyone. Where dignity is concerned, all human beings are radically equal. But from the point of view of their talents, they are radically unequal. Many are those who would be able to work miracles, but who do foolish things because the mob is their only point of reference.

I was aware of the immense talents God had granted me. I did not compare myself to anyone, not to Hauviette nor to Mengette, my childhood friends. I loved them a lot; my sense of justice told me that God could not demand of them what he demanded of me.

Do not let occasions for action pass you by. Letting the opportunity pass, not seizing it out of fear or laziness—this is what makes a magnanimous soul suffer more than anything else. Remember: evil is not what others do, it is the good that you, personally, do not do.

At Vaucouleurs, where I went for the second time to convince Robert de Baudricourt, the royal captain, to take me to the dauphin at Chinon, I did not stand still. I was in a hurry to leave in order to accomplish my mission. I had just turned seventeen and time was weighing on me like a woman wanting to become a mother. Baudricourt was still not taking me seriously, but unlike the first time I met him, this time I had no intention of going back. In the street, I met a young knight, Jean de Metz, and I told him with all the rage that was consuming me, "I came here to ask Robert de Baudricourt to take me to the king, but he paid no attention to me or what I was saying. And yet, I must go before the king before the middle of Lent because he will have no help except through me." I insisted on these last words. It was this young man, thirty-one years of age, who persuaded Baudricourt to embrace my cause and was the head of the small company of troops escorting me to Chinon.

Act as if "no one else can help except you."

One last thing: Remember that the magnanimous person risks everything because he is afraid of losing something greater than everything else combined.

Some practical advice:

Make a list of magnanimous persons (living, deceased, literary personages) to study and be inspired by. Enumerate the internet resources you will use, the books you will read, and the movies you will watch. Which bad "environment" will you turn your back on? Seek a qualified advisor who can help you set magnanimous goals and attain them.

Millais, John Everett,
Joan of Arc (detail), oil on canvas,
1865, private collection.

Five

Cultivate Filial Piety

*You discover little by little your own greatness—
your dignity, your talent. I encourage you to
continue along this path, which is the path of
truth. But there is one thing you should reflect on
frequently: without God, you are nothing.*

The more conscious you are of your personal greatness, the more you should recognize that greatness is a gift from God.

Magnanimity without humility is no magnanimity at all. It is self-betrayal and can easily lead to personal calamities of one kind or another. Your greatness is a gift from God. Your strength is a gift from God. You should offer them up to God and consecrate them to him.

A humble person has his sights fixed on God, who is the inexhaustible source of his being.

I was aware that without God I was nothing. I constantly sought his presence and naturally had recourse to him. I did not confine myself to the requirements religion prescribed. I passionately sought the face of God and communion with him. I was a pious and religious soul from my earliest childhood. I owe my piety to my mother, Isabelle. Everything I knew about Christian life I took from her teaching and example.

Young people mocked me for my religiosity. My friend Mengette often told me I was too pious. I took this reproach as a compliment, which made me blush.

My faith translated into good works. When I had some money, I gave it as alms. I took in the poor and consoled the sick.

At Vaucouleurs, where my adventure began, I attended morning Mass every day and remained long afterwards in prayer. I went down to the subterranean chapel and knelt before an image of Mary, my head bowed down or raised to heaven. Later, at court, praised and glorified by military officers and clerics, I remained the person my mother had made me.

I was *naturally* supernatural. I accomplished the will of God with simplicity. I knew—so my voices had told me—that I would be taken prisoner, but if I had known that this would happen at Compiègne, I would not have gone there. It was not my custom to throw myself into the wolf's maw. God was well aware of the dose of good sense he had granted me; that is why he did not alert me to my capture. My good sense would have been detrimental to his plans. I behaved so naturally that when I was a prisoner of the Burgundians, I tried to escape twice. Should not a prisoner be obliged to try to escape? After the failure of my first attempt to escape the chateau of Beaulieu, I concluded that God did not want me to do it. However, I could not resist a new temptation: I tried again, this time from the chateau of Beaurevoir. I fell twenty meters in the attempt. I ought to have died. God saved me, but he was not happy with me that day, I had to confess.

I was pious, simply and naturally. There was nothing strange or extravagant in me. Mine was a popular religion: I lived from prayer, the gospel, confession, and the Eucharist. I was a girl like any other. I was a good Christian, aware of the power of my baptismal consecration. That is why I liked to assert that I had been "well-baptized." I owed to my baptism my dignity, my strength, my vocation, and the direction of my life. I lived close to God.

Piety begins with the truth. The great truth is that without God, you do not exist. Anyone not understanding this simple fact cannot be humble or pious.

If life is a gift of God, religious indifference is an abomination. If God wanted you to be, justice demands that you love him with all of your heart, all of your mind, and all of your soul. So, I encourage you to be pious. May your piety be that of a child—natural, sincere, and trusting.

Some practical advice:

What is the quality of your relationship with God? How often each day do you recollect yourself in his presence? Do you assiduously seek his face in your ordinary activities? Is your daily prayer the intimate dialogue of a son or daughter with your Father, or is it the impersonal recitation of routine phrases? Create a daily plan of piety adapted to your familial, professional, and social obligations, a plan followed every day whether you are tired or well-rested, whether you have time or not, because this plan is the great strategic priority of your life.

LePage, Jules Bastien, *Joan of Arc* (detail),
oil on canvas, 1879,
Metropolitan Museum of Art, New York, NY.

Six

Help Yourself and Heaven Will Help You

You pray a lot, but you do not do *anything.*

You have to pray, but you also have to act. "Help yourself and heaven will help you." I often repeat these words. They have entered into history. When the theologians of Poitiers asked me why I needed an army if it was the will of God to deliver the French people, I told them, "The soldiers will fight, and God will grant the victory." They were stupefied by the profundity and simplicity of my theology.

In Paris, the king did not want to fight, and this was a disaster. After the coronation at Reims, nothing could have stopped the restoration of the towns of France to

Charles VII, but it was necessary to take Paris at any price. Without it, the possession of other towns would not have lasted or been assured. So, I decided to attack Paris. I was betrayed; at the most propitious moment for our armies, the king decided to retreat. The attack on Paris failed, giving new strength to the English and compromising my authority. I had said that the city would be taken, provided we persevered. At Orléans, before the fortress of Les Tourelles, our captains wanted to retreat after I was struck by an arrow between the neck and shoulder. I dissuaded them, and we took the fortress. Had we done the same thing in Paris we would have had a similar success, despite my having been struck in the leg by an arrow. The king betrayed not only France but also God, who was engaged in this battle.

God counts on us. He rejoices in our victories; he does not want to win all on his own.

The war in which you are engaged is a total war. It is no longer a question of saving France from the English; it is a question of saving humanity from self-destruction. Your world sacrifices the dignity and freedom of millions of human beings on the altar of pleasure every day. Ever more sex, and ever less freedom: this is the great reality of the religion of the belly, foretold in 1880 by Fyodor Dostoevsky in his famous "Legend of the Grand Inquisitor"[7] and Aldous Huxley in 1932 in his *Brave New World*. The West is conducting a relentless war on the Creator and his creation.

It is the last war, because the technological revolution is rendering the unimaginable imaginable.

It is not enough to know these things and to pray. You must act and strike at the very heart of the enemy's power. Your responsibility is vast. Your silence is deadly. What you call prudence is nothing but pusillanimity and cowardice.

Because of your silence, you will soon forfeit your right to think for yourself. You will be hunted down until you enthusiastically and warmly embrace all of Big Brother's delirious obscenities. And like the masses manipulated by the media, you will wind up hating the victim and loving the executioner. You will wind up crucifying Christ, democratically.

Some practical advice:

Passivity, quietism, and escapism—these are some of the ways to defeat the grace of God. If you have a melancholic temperament, you find it a challenge to act. You

---

7   Fyodor Dostoyevsky, "The Grand Inquisitor," chapter 5 of part 2, book 5, in *The Brothers Karamazov* (1879–1880).

are afraid of the unknown. You insist on certainty. Do
not be discouraged. Train yourself to take risks. Make
several bold decisions this year concerning your professional, social, spiritual, and familial life. And do not wait
to carry them out.

Unknown artist, *Joan of Arc miniature* (detail),
gouache and watercolor on paper, c. 1450-1500,
Archives Nationale, Paris, France.

Seven

Put Your Intelligence Into Everything You Do

You trust in God, but you do not think.
You tend to believe that, being pious,
you do not need to be smart.

I never thought that divine wisdom should substitute for my intelligence. I put my heart into my mission, but I never forgot to apply my brains.

From the first hours of my vocation, when I was just a child, I changed nothing about my conduct. No one knew what was happening inside of me, not even the priest hearing my confession. I kept my calling secret to

ensure success when it came time to act. I was afraid of
the trap of the Burgundians and of my father's resistance.
Despite my young age, I saw the reality facing me and
made decisions based on that reality. Nothing required
me to remain silent, but I understood that this was the
best thing to do. And so, I said nothing.

I was perspicacious concerning my vocation and the
war. Contrary to the opinion of the captains, I always
wanted to strike a blow at the heart of English power. Often, they did not want to obey, but they always admitted
I was right. On the battlefield at Orléans, I had to inter-
vene three times to change the plans of the captains, and
my interventions brought us victory. I had worked out a
science of warfare, which was ahead of its time. I knew
how to make use of spears, rally the army, prepare for battle, and deploy artillery. I was most admired for my use
of artillery, for which I had a consummate talent. I was
illiterate, but I was wiser, more prudent and clear-sighted
than all of the combined political and military minds. I
perceived realities, which they did not despite their age
and experience.

I was perceptive and prudent about my vocation, the
war, and, above all, my trial.

I did not allow myself to be deceived by Bishop Cauchon, even when he made a show of affection. Cauchon,
who would have had me stand in a steel cage bound at

the neck, hands, and feet, called me "Joan, my very dear friend." He said to me, "Everything I am doing is for your own good. The most noble aspirations of your heart, the ecstasy of a pious soul, and the exaltation of an ardent patriotism are the source of the illusion, which you are a propagating in good faith."

"My very dear friend," "noble heart," "pious soul, "ardent patriotism," "good faith." . . . Do not let yourself be manipulated by such hypocritical flattery, which is an instrument of the devil. I saw into Cauchon's heart. I pitied him and prayed for him.

I was clairvoyant, quick, and judicious. By a clever tactic, my judges interspersed their questions and constantly changed the subject to get me to contradict myself. However, I had a good memory!

They were determined to know what sign I had given the king at Chinon, so that he could understand that my mission came from God. In order to hide the secret, I fatally confused them with allegories they could not understand.

One of my judges asked me if I was in the grace of God. It was a trick question: if I said no, I would have been lying and admitting that my mission was not from God; if I had said yes, this could have been interpreted as pride. I replied, "If I am not in the grace of God, may God put me there; if I am, may God so keep me, because I would be the saddest creature in the world if I knew I were not in his grace!" The judge remained confused and the officers of the court dumbstruck. They suspended the interrogation to allow the public to catch its breath.

The members of the tribunal were so overwhelmed by the strength and simplicity of my answers that Cauchon, out of fear, closed the public interrogation.

Later, during the prison sessions, I was asked if I deferred to the Church. If I had said yes, I would have been abandoning my mission to the arbitrariness of the judges, who had categorically rejected my appeals to the Pope; if I had said no, I would have been accused of heresy. I replied, "I simply know Our Lord and the Church are one, and we should not complicate the matter. Why are you making trouble about this?" I reminded my judges that Christ should be put first—first serve our Lord— and that the people of the Church should love him rather than crucify him. I did not refuse the judgment of the Church. I accepted it if I could be assured that I would not be judged, under the Church's name, by her very enemies. Cauchon was the enemy of the Church even more than he was the enemy of France: at the council of Basle, several years later, he would accuse not me, but the bishop of Rome, the head of the universal Church, of heresy. He would even try to depose him. In appealing to the Pope, I foresaw that the judgment of condemnation brought against me would be annulled several years later by a tribunal, which the Pope himself would convoke.

Learn from my lucidity, my perspicacity, my presence of mind, the audacity of my language, and my just and simple way of escaping all the traps in this struggle carried out by people of learning, as clever as they were perverse.

> Because of [Wisdom] I shall have glory among the multitudes and honor in the presence of the elders, though I am young. I shall be found keen in judgment, and in the sight of rulers I shall be admired. When I am silent they will wait for me, and when I speak they will give heed; and when I speak at greater length, they will put their hands on their mouths. (Wis 8:10–12)

This text is always the first reading of the Mass the Church celebrates in my memory.

Wisdom is a divine gift requiring a serious effort to practice the human virtue of prudence. I practiced prudence like few people before me. To be prudent, you need an upright heart and a strong will.

Some practical advice:

Prudence does not consist of being cunning, crafty, or clever. It consists of perceiving situations in all their complexity and making decisions conforming to the perception of reality. Prudence entails two essential elements: deliberation and decision. Do you deliberate well? Are you in the habit of confronting reality straight on? Or, do you often "reconstruct" reality, lying to yourself, so as to serve your interests and satisfy your passions? Stated differently, do you manufacture problems to justify desired solutions, or do you seek real solutions to real problems? Are your decisions effective? Do you habitually overcome your fear of mistakes? Do you implement decisions without delay?

Lynch, Albert, *Jeanne d'Arc* (detail),
engraving, 1903, cover of "Figaro Illustré" magazine,
Paris, France.

Eight

Discover Your Mission

You thirst for great things and make bold plans, but God is absent from them. These are your plans, not his. Your piety does not inform your life.

God has a plan for you. Discover this plan and carry it out. This is the great task of your life.

True piety consists above all in listening. It was because I listened to God that I heard my voices. I was thirteen years old. The first time I was very afraid. Two or three times a week, the voices told me to leave for France.[8] When I was sixteen and had to leave, I told my voices that I was a poor girl, who did not know how to ride a

---

8   Joan was born and lived in Domrémy, in the Duchy of Bar on the northeastern border of the Kingdom of France. The part of the duchy, in which she was born, owed fealty to the Crown of France; the other part was under the Holy Roman Empire.

horse or make war. I was afraid mostly of myself, because I knew that once I embarked on my adventure, I would *never* turn back. Because I was pious, I conquered my fear. And from that day, my only thought was to accomplish the will of God. God's will became my obsession. I often said I would rather be dragged by four horses and dismembered than come to France without having done God's will.

My love for France was not the fruit of an extreme patriotism. It is true that my father was a patriot. However, what obsessed me was the will of God. My patriotism did not give birth to my visions; my visions gave birth to my patriotism. My voices advised me to do things I could not imagine; they commanded me to do things I found repugnant.

I felt sorry for the French because God felt sorry for them. I loved France for God. As I told you, my voices named me "Daughter of God." This name resulted in my being burned at the stake. I was condemned as a heretic because I affirmed, without ceasing, that I had been sent by God to do his will. I was not burned as a prisoner of war. They do not burn prisoners of war.

Many would like to make me a symbol of patriotism. That is because they do not, or do not want, to understand me. The Church canonized me very late—five hundred years after the annulment of my trial—to avoid all confusion in this regard. I am not a "patriot." I am someone who loves the will of God.

France will recover once she begins to understand me.

Here is what Jules Michelet, the famous nineteenth-century historian, wrote about me:

> France was until then a collection of provinces, a vast chaos of fiefdoms, a big country, a vague idea. But from that day, on the strength of the heart, it was a *patrie*, a homeland. Beautiful mystery. Touching, sublime! How the immense and pure love of a young heart ignited a whole world, gave it a second life, the authentic life which only love can give . . . . She so loved France! . . . And France, touched, began to love herself . . . . Our homeland was born of the heart of a woman, of her tenderness and tears, of the blood she gave for us.[9]

This is beautiful, well-written, and moving. However, it is a lie. It is a lie because of what it does not say. Michelet wanted to laicize the gospel of Christ, transform Christian messianism into a popular messianism. It is a trick and sacrilege. It was not I who saved France; it was God. And if God had not saved her though me, he would have saved her in some other way.

Even the Duke of Bedford, the head of the English

---

9 Jules Michelet, *Jeanne d'Arc* (1841).

forces, was less naïve than Michelet. Initially certain of victory, he saw all of his hopes confounded—all of his fortresses overrun, his troops defeated in open fields, his garrisons capitulating, and his soldiers, once so proud, completely demoralized. He understood immediately that this was not the work of a "patriot," even a highly gifted one. He understood that a supernatural power was at work and did not hesitate to attribute it to the devil.

If I had been a "patriot," I would not have tended to wounded soldiers—both French and English—with the same care.

If I were above all a "patriot," I would not have wept over the soul of William Glasdale, the English commander at Orléans, who from the top of his fortress called me "the whore of the Armagnacs," and then, in his armor, fell from the walls into the Loire and drowned.

If I were above all a patriot, my name would not have spread through the whole world; men like Winston Churchill, G. K. Chesterton, and Mark Twain would probably never have been interested in my story. I was a gift of God to all of humanity. To make me into the incarnation of nationalist sentiment is not only unjust, it is also blasphemy.

The greatness of my person transcends grand patriotic notions. They try to desacralize me, to present me as "*la France incarnée*"—the incarnation of France—whereas the mark of my mission was chastity, the opposite of what France was, then and now. When, at the age of thirteen, I understood that an angel had spoken to me, I offered God my heart and my body in complete service to him. I chose as my name, *la Pucelle*, the Maid. Although I was beautiful, charming, and elegant, very few people had carnal temptations in my presence. Those who did so never dared to act on them. In my presence, chastity became contagious. I inflamed the hearts of my soldiers with the divine love burning in my soul. While on campaign, to deter the advances of perverse souls, I remained armed day and night; while in prison, I categorically refused to be dressed as a woman.

I was chastity incarnate, much more than France incarnate. I wanted the soldiers to remain, like me, in the grace of God, in whom I sought my strength. I fought vice in them as their most dangerous enemy and the greatest obstacle to victory. I chased away all "camp followers" of the army; there was no place for such women in an army led by invoking the Blessed Virgin, the Mother of God. I reprimanded dukes and princes, just as I did the others. My comrades in arms, my most enthusiastic partisans, resembled beasts more than human beings: La Hire, Xaintrailles, Gilles de Rais. I made thousands of men confess, beginning with La Hire. I only allowed under my banner those living in the state of God's grace;

I ordered soldiers to confess before taking the field of battle. I wanted every soldier to be at peace with his conscience and to live in friendship with Jesus and Mary. I wept for soldiers, whether French or English, who fell in battle without having confessed.

I did not die crying *"Vive la France!"* I died with the name of Jesus on my lips. I shouted his name six times amidst the flames before suffocating from the smoke. I loved France, obviously, but Jesus was the love of my life.

I was a patriot, but it was the will of God I loved above all. The will of God manifests itself in vocation and mission. Vocation is a *call to be*, to think, to act in a particular way; mission is a *call to do* something specific. Although vocation and mission are different things, it can happen that God fuses them. He fused them in my case: I was called—that was my vocation; I was sent— that was my mission.[10] My vocation was my mission.

My mission was given to me directly by God—by the angels, by the voices, by the visions—because he was asking me to depart from the ordinary. For you, things are different. What God expects of you, he communicates through the usual channels of the interior life, not through angels, visions, or voices. Although he uses or-

---

10 *Vocation* comes from the Latin *vocare* (to call), whereas *mission* comes from *mittere* (to send).

dinary means, therein lies their interest. They presume that you will bring to bear your heart, mind, will, imagination, and memory, and that you will free yourself once and for all of the thirst for certainty and security that is devouring you.

I also had doubts. Until the king's coronation at Reims, I had done nothing, which was not the express commandment of God. After Reims, my voices became much less explicit. I wanted to go home, but my heart told me that my mission was not finished. I decided to go into battle without the advice of my voices. I did not know if I would succeed. God decided to leave me to my own devices for several months.

You will always have doubts about your mission and how to accomplish it. If you are pious, God will not abandon you. He will grant you his grace and light, as you make choices bringing you closer to achieving your mission. This mission demands imagination and creativity on your part. Even if it does not descend from heaven, it is an integral part of God's plan for you.

Some practical advice:

In order to discover your mission, you need to know yourself. "Who am I?" You must learn to contemplate your life and your destiny, and to find the right words to talk about it. It is your story, not your whims, which define your mission. It is also the story of those who live in you, in one way or another. Your story is a light allowing you to interpret reality deeply and originally. It is a force impelling you to action. You should formulate your mission in such a way that it clearly accentuates the cultural and social challenge which you are responding to through actions that are passionate and determined. Your mission should be, at the same time, expansive and precise. Expansive, so that you can accomplish it in a variety of ways, and precise, so that you always have it in mind.

Hillingford, Robert Alexander, *Joan of Arc* (detail),
oil on canvas, undated, private collection.

Nine

Do Not Confuse Your Objectives With Your Mission

You set numerous objectives, but you are unable to define the great mission of your life.

Break the siege of Orléans, engineer the coronation of the king at Reims, chase the English out of France. That, it would seem, is a grand mission.

In reality, these were mere objectives; my mission far transcended them. I was born for something sublime: to physically and spiritually uplift a people on whom God had taken pity. I was born to testify to the love of God for France and make this love manifest in the eyes of the world.

From the start of the Christian era, God had never mixed in the affairs of men in the *manner* of men—through blood and arms and fire. Out of love for France, he ran an enormous risk: that of not being understood by Christians themselves. In the Old Testament, there is a place for me—among the judges, the warlords of the Jewish people. But in the New Testament? In the New Testament, there are no Jews, or Canaanites, or Philistines; there are no Frenchmen or Englishmen or Germans. There are only children of God. However, God gave France a young girl after his own heart to direct armies under his banner and repel the English invader. He took sides. In almost two thousand years, the world had seen nothing like it. But God did it out of love for France, so that the whole world would understand his feelings in this regard.

I, Joan, exist to bear witness to God's love of France. That is the meaning of my life and mission, which, by the way, is not over. Many Frenchmen—too many—want to hear nothing about God, about his love, or about France. France is ungrateful. She is rebelling against God, against his love, against herself, despite the talents she has received and the mercy she was shown.

It is through me, once again, that she must rise up. My objectives I achieved long ago, but my mission is eternal. When I was thirteen years old, my voices insistently told me to "go to France." I am still going to France and will not cease to do so, to remind the French that God is tirelessly extending them his hand. That is my mission.

The great majority of human beings never discover their mission, because they do not seek it. They lack the depth to carry out this task. At best, they set some more attainable objectives. Their intelligence is satisfied, their desires slaked by attaining certain concrete and quantifiable goals; however, their hearts remain empty.

Your mission will be fulfilled through the achievement of concrete objectives, but it must transcend those objectives. You are your mission. Your mission is a synthesis. If you live it intensely, it is etched in your face.

Remind yourself of these words of Rainer Maria Rilke: "Your life is strong, but even stronger is your song."[11] Your song is your mission—it is the life your heart has chewed over and over, until it has squeezed it, ground it up, and drained it of its unique content. Your song is your life deciphered. It is the idea, which you and you alone incarnate.

Your song is expressed in a few words, or perhaps just one. It is a symbol.

Your song—it is your heart that must sing it.

---

11 Rainer Maria Rilke, *Musik.*

Some practical advice:

You have set your objectives and were right to do so. After all, a mission without objectives is not worth very much. Rest assured: beyond these objectives, there is a mission giving them a meaning. If, by temperament, you are rather choleric, you tend to concentrate all of your attention on material objectives, on "management." Learn to look farther, and, above all, higher.

Américo de Figueiredo e Melo, Pedro, *Joan of Arc Listening for the First Time to the Voices That Predict Her Prominent Fate* (detail), oil on canvas, 1884, Museu Nacional de Belas Artes, Rio de Janeiro, Brazil.

Ten

Work for the Long Term

You crave immediate results. You want to be rewarded on the spot for your efforts. You cannot wait. You have a hard time working for the long term. You seem effective, but seen over time, it is clear you are pretty useless.

It is always great when your efforts bear immediate results. I had this experience.

In four days of combat, I broke the siege of Orléans, which lasted seven months.

In less than a week, I chased the English from their main positions on the Loire and defeated them on open fields as they retreated.

In less than a month, I led the king from Chinon to

Reims, with an army deprived of everything, through land occupied by the enemy.

In less than a year, I overcame the rebuffs of de Baudricourt at Vaucouleurs, even though when he first saw me, he ordered my uncle to slap me a few times and send me as quickly as possible back to my mother.

In record time, I overcame the distrust of the king at Chinon, the theologians at Poitiers, the military officers at Orléans, and the politicians at Reims.

That is what I did. I was only seventeen years old. No one could accuse me of being a "dreamer," an "idealist," or a "theoretician."

Look closely and you will see that these results, remarkable in the eyes of the world, have no great value in themselves. The moment of my triumph—the anointing of the king, which consecrated him in the eyes of the French people—in reality marked a sharp setback for me personally. To be sure, the king ennobled me and my parents and brothers "in recognition of my services." However, I was not duped. I understood what it meant: it was the thank-you gift to someone you want to get rid of, the medal given an old soldier on the eve of retirement. The king, for whom I had done so much, had abandoned me. I had become an obstacle to his court, which was interested in nothing but living in peace with the Burgundian traitors working for the English. Because the king abandoned me, Paris was not taken. This defeat broke the spirit of the royal army and undermined the strategic significance of all our previous victories.

Immediate results are relative. To change the world, we must learn to work for the long term. I worked for the long term. What counts is what is happening in souls. And things were happening. I transformed the hearts of several million people and provoked the spiritual renewal of a nation, which had sunk into mediocrity and darkness. The people regained their confidence. Whereas formerly, two hundred Englishmen had routed eight hundred soldiers of the king's army; at Orléans, four hundred of our soldiers dared to brave all of the English forces.

The immediate results only mean something if they trigger an irreversible process. I wanted immediate results because I knew—thanks to my voices—that I would only last a single year. These immediate results were necessary to the accomplishment of my mission.

Do not worry if material results are late in coming. Focus on your mission. It is moving forward in the hearts of men. It can take several decades to complete a mission. The important thing is not to abandon the arena.

Some practical advice:

Do you bring a long-term perspective to what you do? Do you seek the common good of humanity or only your short-term interests and personal satisfaction? Do you regularly analyze the results of your work in light of your mission? If you have a sanguine temperament, thinking and acting over the long term can be a challenge for you. You easily undertake new projects, enjoying the adventure and diversion they bring, but you have a hard time bringing them to a conclusion because you hate routine. Do not be discouraged. Learn to practice patience, perseverance, and faithfulness.

Pichore, Jean, *Saint Joan of Arc*, miniature illumination on vellum (detail), 1504-1506, in *Antoine Dufour's The Lives of Famous Women*, Ms. 17, folio 76 verso, Musée Dobrée, Nantes, France.

Eleven

Flee Voluntarism

*You do the will of God because you "have to."
You do things because you "have to" and only
because you have to. Your heart is suffocated by
your will. You banish from your behavior any sort
of emotion, so that only your will remains.*

You are a voluntarist, and probably think I was, too. You think I submitted coldly to God's will like the heroine in a Greek tragedy, who submits stoically to her fate.

I am not a stoic but a Christian. I loved the will of God more than I submitted to it. I rejoiced in his will much more than in my submission to it. I did good with my will, most certainly, but I did it also and above all with my heart—with my feelings and emotions, with my senses and flesh. I had learned from earliest childhood to revel in the good. I knew sorrow, but I learned to discover charm, transcendence, and mystery in every moment.

I was a very physical being. I was far from being diminutive, frustrated, or alienated. I lived my story with passion.

In action, I felt the joy of God. I *was* the joy of God. I put my heart into everything I did. I did things well and did them with grace. It was not only the results, which interested me.

At Orléans, before the attack, I begged Bedford not to force me to destroy him. I said that if he came to terms with me, I would put on a big celebration and let him enjoy my company. My very noble offer drove Bedford, a very perverse individual, half-crazy.

The human and superhuman intensity of my personality captivated men. Warriors followed me even at the risk of ridicule. During the Loire campaign, near Jargeau, the Duke of Alençon, who was the lieutenant general of the king and my comrade-in-arms, hesitated before attacking. He thought it was too early and that we were not ready. I approached him and whispered in his ear, "Oh, gentle Duke, are you afraid? Didn't you know I promised your wife I would bring you back safe and sound?" My words sufficed to get him going. We attacked and routed the English, capturing their commander, the Duke of Suffolk.

I was endowed with an uncommon will. My actions show that. However, I was no voluntarist. It was my heart, above all, that made me who I am.

Your heart is the core of your personality, the sacred place of your inner self. Your heart gives your will its primary orientation. Without it, all acts of the will are just a headlong rush into the dark. The strength of your virtues depends on the purity of your heart, even more than on the strength of your will.

Remember: your personal value depends on the quality of your affectivity, and not on your ability to subsume your affectivity to your will.

Some practical advice:

Learn to be happy. Be convinced that happiness is not a sin! Refuse to base your life on things that have nothing to do with you, your interests or nature, and which serve a task or moral obligation existing only in your imagination. Know yourself; discover your own substance and God's will for you. Love God, love yourself, and love others in your *own* way. Learn to live.

Boulaye, Paul de la,
Sainte Jeanne d'Arc (detail)*,* oil on canvas,
1909, private collection.

Twelve

Banish Sentimentalism

You are afraid of confrontations. You say you do not want to make other people suffer. The result is sad: you are not accomplishing your mission.

To do what God was demanding of me, I had no fear of making my parents suffer. I even left the house without their consent, secretly. It was an incredible thing to do in those days; I was only seventeen years old! Because God demanded it, if I had had a hundred fathers and a hundred mothers or if I had been the daughter of the king, I would have left.

Several months before, my parents, worried by what was going on with me, even arranged my engagement. I equivocated; I disobeyed them; I promised nothing to anyone because the plans of men could not take precedence over those of God.

I loved my parents dearly, but I loved them for God, not for themselves. I suffered for them because they did not understand my behavior. I considered this suffering inevitable.

The sentimental person has a heart too "good" to be able to really do good, a heart too "loving" to be able to really love. Make your will more manly. Do not renounce the good on the pretext that it could give rise to conflict. Do not be cowardly. Learn to manage conflicts with sincerity and firmness.

"Well, it's just that . . . mother is against it." Forget about mother! Don't let your heart absorb your will.

You live in a world in which a handful of terrorists are able to conduct a pitiless war against everything constituting the moral and spiritual heritage of humanity. And you, in the face of this satanic and totalitarian will, when it comes to the accomplishment of your mission, are afraid to hurt people by your conduct and your words?

Your gentleness, modesty, and humility are acts of cowardice and hypocrisy.

I wish you knew the strength and words I used to correct my comrades-in-arms, when I saw them weakening. It was not easy for me, but I had a horror of sentimentalism. I often cried, but that did not prevent me from taking action. I was the teacher of a nation because I was not afraid to speak, to correct, and, when I had to, to get angry.

Some practical advice:

Examine yourself. Sentimentalism is the fruit of cowardice. You are afraid to experience an unpleasant moment. This is also the fruit of hypocrisy: you say you do not want to make others suffer, but in reality, it is you who do not want to suffer. Learn to be sincere with yourself and with others.

Chapu, Henri, *Jeanne d'Arc à Domrémy*,
marble, 1836-38,
d'Orsay Museum Paris, France.

Thirteen

Purify Your Intentions

You get all wound up and go charging off in all directions because you are afraid of not being noticed. You need to have others recognize your talent. You crave applause.

Why? Could it be because you have little sense of your dignity and worth in the eyes of God? Do you really think your worth depends on your accomplishments and on what others say about them?

Your vanity is the fruit of stupidity. You are worth more in the eyes of God than the sum of all the applause of the most remarkable people who ever lived on this earth.

I never sought applause. It was enough for me to know that God loved me. The one who possesses a profound sense of personal dignity does not need applause. Our exterior activity is the extension of our interior richness; it is not determined by vanity.

The positive things people say about you are worth nothing. What God says about you is what counts. God alone speaks well of you. So, purify your intentions. Get rid of all pride, vanity, and thirst for recognition. Concentrate on the will of God and forget yourself.

I lived a life of action not to be acclaimed but to accomplish the will of God. I drove, I pressured, and I attacked. I could not stand laggards. The word, *delay,* did not exist in my vocabulary. I had no qualms and no doubts. I thirsted for action, not in order to be admired but to do the will of God. The will of God was that the English go home. After the coronation of the king at Reims, I would willingly have returned to my meadows to take care of my sheep alongside my mother, father, and brothers. I had had enough of those pusillanimous and calculating politicians, always ready to betray. However, I continued my struggle because that is what God wanted.

I sought the will of God, not glory. I was a daughter of God and that was enough for me. I was applauded several times, but mainly I was betrayed and abused. The conduct of the French court was one of unparalleled baseness and ingratitude. When I was made prisoner of the Burgundians, no attempt was made to free me by launching a surprise attack. There was no attempt to ransom me for money or to outbid the offer of the English; there were no negotiations with the Duke of Burgundy, whose opposition had softened markedly and who had accepted offers of a truce and would make peace. While I was prisoner of the English, there was no letter from the bishop of Reims, chancellor of France,[12] to the bishop of Beauvais, his suffragan and the ringleader of the trial, to at least apprise him of the procedure; neither was there an effort by the king to petition the Holy Father. I was deliberately abandoned to my fate. The king and his entourage appropriated to themselves the fruits of my victories; they blamed me for setbacks of their own making. The English, defeated by me, were less guilty of my death than the French, whom I saved, and who then did nothing to save *me*.

I was maltreated by the world, but never lost my interior peace, which comes from our relationship with God. So, do not worry if those who ought to acclaim you ignore or insult you. Seek to please God alone.

Some practical advice:

Examine your intentions. Why do you feel the need to be recognized? Could it be that you lack a sense of your

---

12 The chancellor of France was a high official of the Crown. He was named by the king and charged with the administration of justice throughout the realm.

own dignity? Being recognized and honored has nothing to do with the greatness of man. Greatness is achieved through virtue. Vanity takes over the moment recognition becomes, even if only secondarily, the reason to act. We can destroy this subtle vanity and achieve perfect purity of intention only through long, hard work. How are you doing in this endeavor?

Unknown Artist, steel engraving (detail), c.1821,
in *L'Orléanide: poème national en vingt-huit chants*
by Philippe-Alexandre Le Brun de Charmettes.

Fourteen

Have No Fear of Public Opinion

You pay too much attention to your image.

You are right not to neglect your image. It would be wrong to be indifferent to the impression you make. The efficacy of your work depends on this impression. It is important that many people take an interest in what you do and say. If you want to change the world, you will need all of the advantages you can muster—and image is one of them. Not attending to your image is a lack of professionalism. It is also a lack of common sense.

I attended to my image. My horse, my armor, my sword, my standard, and my posture . . . everyone admired my grace when mounted, my military bearing. I was truly "presentable." I had a remarkable charm. People were eager to see me.

If you do things well and with elegance, it is normal that you will win friends. It is also to be expected that you will make enemies. If the whole world praises you and lauds your merits, ask yourself serious questions about the importance and efficacy of your actions, because you may well be wasting your time.

It was because I did things well and accomplished good that I was insulted, hunted down, and lynched by the intellectuals of the time. During my trial, I had all the judges and court officials, with the exception of a few for the sake of appearances, as well as all of the media and those who represent science against me. I was in the most absolute moral and psychological isolation.

I was alone, without legal representation, contrary to the practice of the Inquisition. I faced a tribunal of a hundred angry men chosen by enemies to be my judges. I was also alone in facing the hatred of the academics of the University of Paris, who not only presumed to govern the universal Church in place of the Pope but also to legitimize the English conquest of France. They declared my revelations mendacious, subversive, and inspired by the devil. They accused me of idolatry and blasphemy. They complimented Bishop Cauchon, their former rector, for his zeal, praised his conduct of the trial and its "conformity to the law." They even recommended that the bishop, in his paternal solicitude, overlook nothing until "he avenged the divine majesty for my insults." They praised the King of England for the ardor he had shown on this occasion "in defending the faith and extirpating error."

So much science, so many titles, and so many magnificent minds aimed against me!

The trial was not Stalinist. It was not led by puppets. Although ferocious, the trial was "democratic," led by vain intellectuals incapable of questioning their own prejudices. The burden of proof was on me, the victim! I had to demonstrate my innocence.

I confronted the cream of the European intelligentsia of the time, infatuated by their own poor knowledge. Nothing protected me. I should have succumbed morally. I should have had serious doubts. I weakened for a while under the weight of the ordeal, but I regrouped.

The English were accused later of having been the authors of this abominable spectacle; in reality, it was mainly the work of the French.

If you do good, lasting and effective good, it is not surprising that you will be slandered and that some media will take practice shots with you as the target. Your image will be "democratically" sullied and dragged through the mud; you will be "democratically" crucified.

It is important that you be warned, because the shock is brutal and the chances of survival for those not expecting it are practically nonexistent.

Some practical advice:

Does the image you give of yourself correspond to reality? Do you take care that the impression you make faithfully reveals your intentions, virtues, and talents? Are you doing too much, or not enough? Are you prepared to sacrifice your image in the name of truth and the good, in the name of your conscience?

LeJeune, Boris, *Jeanne d'Arc à l'Ermitage de Bermont*,
marble, 2013, Velaux, France.

Fifteen

Reject
Perfectionism

In your personal struggle to follow the advice I
am giving you, you may often fall. You may become
demoralized, discouraged, and struggle to get back
on your feet. You want your way to be perfect; you
want to be rewarded for good behavior. You do not
accept failure. When you fail, you feel humiliated
and are ready to give up the fight.

Your perfectionism is the fruit of pride. You cannot accept
not being perfect. You think you are so strong and smart!
And there you are, flat on your face. You despair when you
see that you are not what you want to be.

Be convinced that the important thing is not to never
fall, but to always get back on your feet with humility

and simplicity. Behave like a professional athlete, who never gets discouraged and begins again after each failure with renewed enthusiasm. You need the simplicity and flexibility of a child, who after having stumbled, bounces back like a rubber ball. Consider each day to be a new chapter in your life.

It is normal to fall. I fell several times. Think of my attempt to flee the chateau of Beaurevoir. I wanted to escape to aid the inhabitants of Compiègne, even though I knew that God had other plans for me. I had a hard time accepting that reality. Instead of falling into despair for having disobeyed, I confessed and continued along my way—to my imprisonment and death in Rouen—in all simplicity and without making a drama of it.

Think of my "recantation" at the cemetery at Saint-Ouen several days before my martyrdom. In this cemetery, on a scaffold, face-to-face with my judges, surrounded by the crowd, escorted by court bailiffs and solicitors, I experienced the most terrible moral assault of my life. I was exhausted. I could not go on. My body, accustomed to the open air and created for action, had been imprisoned for a year. For six months, I had been handcuffed during the day and chained at night. I was at the end of my physical strength. And, afraid of the stake, I submitted—unwillingly—to my judges. I signed a document I poorly understood, and which was interpreted as a recantation on my part. They had set me a trap: they promised that if I signed, I would be transferred from my civil prison, where I had been chained in contravention of canon law and severely mistreated by my jailers, to an ecclesiastical prison with presumably better conditions. This was a trap; I was not strong enough to evade it. God made me understand that I should not have signed the document. I asked his pardon, my spirits rebounded, and I denied before my judges that I had recanted in any way. I took back none of my testimony. This act is called the "relapse" and was the juridical cause of my death at the stake.

I had made a mistake. I had weakened, but I rebounded with new energy, more convinced than ever of the truth within me. God transformed my weakness into victory and reduced the time of my ordeal. He put an end to this miserable trial within a few days and received my soul in glory.

Be humble and simple so you will always rise again. It is normal to fall. It is not normal not to rise again.

Some practical advice:
Are you demoralized by failure? Are you overwhelmed by your mistakes, weaknesses, and shortcomings? At the end of each day, put your miseries in the hands of God. Submerge yourself in his mercy. Forget the past. Renew

yourself. Get up each morning with a healthy enthusiasm, which is not a reflection of naivete, but of a warrior spirit full of faith, hope, and charity.

Postscript

In making Joan your coach, you cannot go wrong. Joan, as you will have noticed, is a universal model accessible to all men and women, whatever their cultural or religious background.

The interest Joan arouses today in all parts of the world comes as no surprise. The heroine of Orléans is an astonishingly modern woman. There is nothing strange about her, nothing inappropriate or anachronistic. Joan is eternally new.

The "Case of Joan of Arc" is unique in history. We know everything about her life, even though it was lived in the fifteenth century. Nothing we know about her is the stuff of legend; our knowledge is based on archival documents.

God wanted it to be so. He wanted Joan to be for all of us—men and women working at the very heart of society and worldly affairs—a coach, a teacher, and a mother.

May 16, 2020
Centennial of Joan of Arc's canonization

Chronology of the Life of Joan of Arc

1338   Start of the Hundred Years' War between France and England.

1412   January 6. Birth of Joan of Arc at Domrémy. Domrémy was part of France when Joan was born. It did not belong to Lorraine—part of the Holy Roman Empire of the German Nation—until 1571.

1415   August 13. Exploiting both the lunacy of the King of France, Charles VI, and the incessant quarreling among his advisors, the King of England Henry V lands with his army in Harfleur, Normandy.

October 25. Battle of Agincourt. The French forces, despite superior numbers, are routed by the English.

1420   May 21. The Treaty of Troyes, giving France to the English, is signed by Henry V of England and Charles VI of France. It stipulates that, after the death of Charles, the crown would pass to Henry, who had married Charles' daughter, Catherine of Valois. Thus, Charles disinherits his son, the *dauphin* Charles, the future King Charles VII. Charles VII is stripped of all his titles but remains, *de facto*, head of the government of the south of France.

1422   October 21. Death of Charles VI, two months after the death of Henry V of England. Henry's son is proclaimed King of France and England under the name of Henry VI. He is ten months old. All of the rest of France, including Paris, rallies to Henry VI. The Duke of Bedford, nephew of Henry V, assures the regency in France.

1425   Summer. Joan is thirteen years old. For the first time, she hears voices from God while in her father's garden. These voices ask her to liberate the Kingdom of France from the invader and arrange for the coronation of the *dauphin,* Charles.

1428   May 13. Joan's first meeting with Robert de Baudricourt, the royal captain, at Vaucouleurs. Joan, aged sixteen, asks to go to the *dauphin* Charles at Chinon. Baudricourt does not take her seriously.

October 12. Bedford lays siege to Orléans, the last town north of the Loire loyal to the *dauphin*.

1429   January. Joan's second meeting with Baudricourt at Vaucouleurs.

February 12. Joan's third meeting with Baudricourt at Vaucouleurs.

February 22. Leaving Vaucouleurs for Chinon, Joan is escorted by a small contingent led by Jean de Metz.

March 6. Joan is received by the *dauphin* Charles at Chinon.

March 11. Joan is interrogated at Poitiers. Charles, suspecting Joan might be a witch, makes her submit to an interrogation by the theologians of the University of Poitiers and an examination to establish her virginity and moral uprightness.

May 8. Joan breaks the siege in Orléans. The English commander, William Glasdale, falls from the walls of the fortress into the Loire and drowns.

June 12. The Loire Campaign begins. Jargeau is taken. The Count of Suffolk is taken prisoner by the French.

June 15. Battle of Meung-sur-Loire.

June 16. Battle of Beaugency.

June 18. Battle of Patay. The English general, John Talbot, is taken prisoner by the French. France dislodges England's entire military presence along the Loire.

July 17. The coronation of Charles VII at Reims.

September 8. Joan's failed attack on Paris.

1430   May 23. Joan is taken prisoner by the Burgundians near Compiègne.

June. Joan attempts to escape from the *château de Beaulieu*.

July-October. Joan attempts to escape from the *château de Beaurevoir*.

December 23. Joan, a prisoner, arrives in Rouen.

1431   January 9. The first day of Joan's trial.

May 24. Joan's "recantation."

May 28. Joan resumes dressing like a man. The charge of relapse is introduced.

May 30. Joan is burned alive in Rouen's Old Market Square.

1455-46 Nullification trial. At the request of Joan's mother, Isabelle Romée, Pope Callixtus III orders a review of the trial. The judgment, which is pronounced on July 7, 1456, twenty-five years after Joan's death, declares the first trial "to have been and to be null, void, invalid, worthless, and without effect;" this entirely rehabilitates Joan and her family. Most of the judges from the first trial, including Bishop Cauchon, had since died.

1869   The bishop of Orléans, Msgr. Félix Dupanloup, asks Pope Pius IX to open the process of canonization of Joan of Arc.

1909   April 18. Joan is beatified by Pope Saint Pius X.

1920   May 16. Joan is canonized by Pope Benedict XV.